The

Journey

Rell the Writer

Printed in the United States of America

First Printing, 2021

ISBN 9781708185992

www.rell-the-writer.com

MY PRAYER FOR YOU

Father God,

Only you are holy. Only you are mighty. Only you are wonderful. You are our refuge and our strength a very present help in time of trouble. You are the giver of all things good and our protector from evil. We praise you for your goodness, your loving kindness, your tender mercy, and your grace that is and will always be sufficient.

Lord, we confess that we are sinners and we are blessed to live under your grace through our faith in Jesus Christ. Father, we pray that you will forgive us for sinning against your will and your way for us. Help us to turn from our wicked ways and to seek you always.

We thank you for all the blessings you have continued to shower down upon us. For the blessing of life, of strength, of comfort, or healing, of prosperity, of relationships, of fellowship, of hope, of peace. Father, we thank you for carrying and keeping us through trials and tribulations that have strengthened our character and have given us a wealth of wisdom that we can carry with us as we continue to live the life you blessed us with.

Lord, I pray for the person reading this. I thank you for their life. I thank you for leading them to these words and I pray that the words you have inspired me to put on paper blesses them. I pray over their families and their friends. I pray over the house of worship that they praise you in. I pray over their jobs and their homes and everywhere else they go. Please manifest your presence there and be in the midst as they walk from day to day.

Dear God, I pray that if my dear brother or sister that is reading this right now does not know you like they should or has not accepted the sacrifice of Jesus Christ for the free pardon of their sin; that you will draw them near to you. That they be blessed to accept the free gift for the salvation of their souls and the gain of eternal life.

Bless them, dear Lord. Lift them up and shine your light upon them. And we thank you and praise you for what you've already done, what you're doing, and what you will do.

In the precious and mighty name of JESUS CHRIST, I pray.

Amen.

ACKNOWLEDGEMENTS

First giving honor to my Lord and Savior Jesus Christ. Jesus is the reason I am alive today and He is the reason I am who I am. The greatest gift I ever received is salvation and the only way to salvation is through Jesus Christ. My salvation is why I can write this second book of poems.

I want to thank my wonderful husband, Leo. He has listened to me read him endless poems as he lay in bed at midnight trying to sleep. He has been patient with me as I had to forego quality time in order to write and finalize this book. He has been more than understanding at times when I stopped whatever we were doing because an inspiration hit me. He has been such a blessing when it came to busying the kids; allowing me to focus. Most importantly though, he has always been my biggest supporter. He has always been my biggest cheerleader pushing me toward my goals and holding me accountable. Thank you, Leo, from the bottom of my heart and I love you.

A special thank you to my beautiful daughters, Princess and Sadie. To know the feeling of unconditional love and support is like none other and that is what they give to me. I thank Princess for being honest as she lets me down in the nicest way when she does not like or understand what I wrote. And I want to thank Sadie for her unwavering kindness as she gently tells me how I could have done it better. I mostly appreciate how you always listen when you're asked to give mommy quiet time and space to work. I love you and the spirits God gave you. You are the world's BEST daughters!

I would also want to thank my mom, Barbara. She holds the title as #1 fan! Not only has she been my biggest fan from birth, but she has always encouraged me to be the best I could be. She has never failed to support any endeavor I attempted and has always been there to encourage me to keep pushing if it failed. I especially appreciate her honest feedback. Thank you, Mommy, for everything. You are my queen.

I would like to thank my dad, Freddie. No matter where life took me, he was always there. I thank you, Daddy, for your love, support and your willingness to be available for me.

I would like to thank my family who always supports me in everything I do. By blood, by marriage, or by love, you are all my family and one of the reasons I can keep going. In this section, I have to especially thank two people. Neet, you already know. Thank you. And my best friend, Kristina. Thanks for always having my back, front, and both sides. And of course, I thank the virtuous women of Alpha Theta Omega Christian Sorority, Inc. I love you all!

I must thank Pastor Stephen L. Wright, Sr. and First Lady Linda Wright, or as I would say *my* pastor and first lady! When you look up support in the dictionary their pictures should be there. I am so thankful for their willingness to listen to me vent and rant and clear the thoughts in my head. I appreciate all their advice over the years. I appreciate them helping me work toward being a better person. A person couldn't ask for a better pastor and first lady. I love you with all my heart.

Thank you so much also to the family at First Baptist Church of College Park, the family at Washington Baptist Seminary (and all of the wonderful classmates I met there), and the family at Wilbur Henry Water School of Religion (and all of the wonderful classmates I met there). I have gathered great inspiration from all of you.

I would like to say thank you to my relatives and other people in the world who have made my life difficult and contentious. In order to truly appreciate the good, you must experience the bad. Thank you for being my experience. I have found peace and growth in forgiveness and I continue to pray for you.

Thank you to everyone who takes the time to read and understand these poems. They are from the heart and my prayer is that you are blessed through them.

Remember:

I love you, God loves you more... So, Love Him Back!

~Rell the Writer

RELL THE WRITER'S TESTIMONY: DARKNESS

Darkness.

Darkness all around, whirlpool spinning and spiraling.

Me. Standing in the middle watching in admiration.

The world has me confused.

She is mesmerizing, fantastic and brand new, dressed in fine garments and glimmering diamonds that no girl can refuse.

Right starts to lose the battle to wrong and the thin line between love and hate doesn't seem so strong.

Importance of time becomes a figment of imagination and the only concern is how long until the next welcomed dose of frustration.

Darkness.

Waves of darkness crashing against the shore.

Me. Swimming farther and farther to the point of no return.

The world has me trapped.

She gives sweet, whispered promises of love, success, fun and thrill and delivers these sweet treasures under the guise of God's will.

Justification becomes an everyday excuse and the voice in the back of my head is smothered and put out of use.

Rock bottom gets real close and then BOOM it hits hard and loud. But a small still voice from the deep of my subconscious says, "Turn your head up to the clouds".

Darkness.

The fog of darkness tries to prolong it's stay.

Me. Finding the old light I once used to guide me through the thickness.

The world is chasing after me.
Some who claim to guide have two personas that switch
with no delay and I learn to put on the sweet face and broad
smile at 11 on Sunday.
She builds a tricky fence that sits low enough to straddle,
because everyone else in this world does it with no hassle.
But then God; grabs hold of me. I try brush Him off, but
God grabs a hold of me! Banging on the door to my heart
yet His tone sweet and soft.

Darkness.
Darkness is giving way to the light of a new morning.
Me. Looking around and wondering if I can really be saved
from her.
The world is losing me.
She cries out to me through many a lost soul and
unbelievably, but believably, some who are thought to be
on the path to the goal.
My interests change and my goals become clear as I reach
for the Lord's hand and allow Him to
draw me near.
Change starts to happen and I'm not even aware, but God
has been allowing these trials so that for this, I'd be
prepared
My choices become what He already knows and the right
people are put in place as He works out my deepest woes.

Darkness fading.
The dawn of a new day.
Darkness is no longer the swirling whirlpool of enticing but
disastrous, appealing but dangerous illusion of ecstasy I
once knew.

The world is not darkness. The world is just full of a dark force that no one can handle alone.

I am no longer controlled by the regret of my darkness as I understand I needed it to grow, and the fear of the dark is wiped away when I walk with the One that I know.

Jesus! My Jesus. He also experienced the night, for God's good and perfect will in His life
allows Him to be our Light!

God is so clever in His infinite wisdom that he made man in the image of Him, so like Jesus cut through dark with His light, we must let His light shine from within.

Darkness.
Not a trap, but a testimony.
Not for your worry, but for God's glory.

TABLE OF CONTENTS

PROLOGUE- THE BATTLE   13

PART ONE- THE BEGINNING-
From the World to the Way

Apathetic	18
Dear God	21
Transformation	22
Dear World	24
Questions, Comments, Concerns	25
She Walked Away	31

PART TWO- THE MIDDLE-
Sinner Saved by Grace

The Call	34
Dear Flesh	36
But God	40
Overcomer	43
I Don't Know How to Praise You	46

PART THREE- THE PURPOSE-
The Great Commission

Dear You	50
Don't Forget About God	53
Change Your Mind	55
Let Me Lead You	56

THE LAYOVER   58

= end

PROLOGUE- THE BATTLE

You can't do it. It won't work.
You're not good enough. You'll never measure up.

Here we go, they're at it again
Vicious and mean like-a like-a-a diva, tryna steal my fame
Like a monster hiding under my bed, ready to pounce when
the lights go out
Like the bully in my ear, trying to make me feel bad about
myself.

They're coming for me again and I know that I should fight
back, but…
Sometimes the attack is hard to combat because… well…
its true.

I mean really… come on, really
Who knows anything about me?
The only people who applaud my "talent" are a faithful few
And the church folk just say "good job" because they're
church folk and that's what they do
Who am I kidding…

I'm not good enough.
Just goin' give up, not even going to try…
Just give it a good cry
And crawl back to my mediocre
      Facebook posting,
         Instagram scrolling,
           Podcast recording style…

Hey… **But. God.**

Nah Rell, don't even try it. God aint got nothing to do with this. This is just about your endless need to find purpose.

No. God said that I…

No, don't finish. It's all just a waste of time. You tried and failed and tried and failed… No difference here.

God said I have a gift! And he gave it to me. It's mine!

Girl. This aint it, give it up! You got a gift, but not this. I mean even as you write right now, you're wondering if you should put down the pen.

I'm believing God.

Over me? But, I'm you! And our plans just don't include you trying so hard. Because you'll try and the door will close and you'll be all sad and I mean, haven't we been through that before?

Jesus Christ! I can't take this. I can't win without your help…
I give up… I quit… I'm done. They're right anyway, I always fail.

But God said that he knows the plans that **He** has for me and they include a future and a hope.

And **He** told me to be confident that the works **He's** doing in me won't be cut short.

So, I rebuke you Satan and I rebuke your work.
There's no power in your words.
You're a liar and I have the power because here the Spirit dwells
And in Him, I'll never fail!

You show me all my faults because you want me to be defeated!

...But God...

He shows me my enemies, even when it's only my reflection.
So, I trust Him.
He opens doors and I walk through them and the closed ones get passed by.

But see, I know that closed doesn't always mean it's over, because sometimes he gives me the key.
Like "not right now" doesn't means never and "no, my child", may not mean no forever.

You can't trick me Satan and you won't win because my Spirit is ready for war!
And my flesh can't take the victory this time because my heart wields the sword!

God already stated His purpose, so I know it'll come to light.
Like the words to this poem formed so perfectly in my mind.

So, no matter if man approves or not, I'll know God's will is right.
Because I **know** my merchandise is good.
So, my lamp won't go out by night.

Rell the Writer- Psalm 31:18

The way that you talk to yourself is very impactful to the progress you will make towards God's purpose for you. Practice positive self-talk. You are unique. You are chosen. You are a child of God. You were created for a purpose.

PART ONE:

THE BEGINNING

FROM THE WORLD TO THE WAY

APATHETIC

I don't care.
That's what I said when they asked me if I wanted to go to church anymore.
I know that God is real and maybe, I should go, but I don't really care if I don't.
I care about my life and my soul and often times I wonder what happens next.
But do I want to go to church anymore? I shrug and say, "I don't care".

I don't care for the people staring at me and determining what they can judge next.
I don't care for the gossiper's fake smile trying to give me a façade of concern only to make me the topic of their after service banter.
I don't care for the self-righteous criticism telling me that the way I dress determines my spirituality and the way I talk determines my worthiness.
I don't care for the lying tongue that tells me they've been praying for me right after I had to remind them what my name is.
I don't really care to watch the same sister that mean mugged me and didn't speak this morning jump up and shout glory to God when the piano hits the right notes.
I don't really care to hear the preaching that so effortlessly perverts God's sacred word to further an agenda that they thought was hidden.

I don't care.
That's what I said when they asked me if I wanted to go to church anymore.
I know that God is real and maybe, I should go, but I don't really care if I don't.
I care about my life and my soul and often times I wonder what happens next.
But do I want to go to church anymore? No. I want to be the church and go to worship.

I want to fellowship with people who are looking to come together to praise God, not the preacher, not the deacons, not the officers, not the family that we all know *really* calls the shots.
I want to pray with people who want to know the details only so their prayers can be specific.
I want to pray with the people who know what to say out loud and what to keep in their secret closet.
I want to talk to people who will look for the blessing in my circumstance and help me see it too.
I want to grow with people who know they're messed up, just like me. Who know that even when they have it all together, they're still messed up.
I want to hear God's word so I can be taught, be enlightened, be inspired, be corrected, be filled with joy and hope.

They asked me if I wanted to go to church anymore.
I told them I don't care to go to church, I care to be the church.
I wonder if they know there's a difference. I wonder if they care.

DEAR GOD

I decided to write you a letter,
Although I know praying is enough.
I figured it'd make me feel better,
Because lately, times have been rough.

I mean to say times have been tough,
Tougher than they usually are.
My mind is just cluttered with stuff,
And it seems to push you so far.

They say that my thoughts seem bizarre,
That you're God and you're always near.
But my heart still wears a faint scar,
Of pain, of rejection, of loneliness and of fear.

In you, Lord, my trust still remains, in you it will always
be.
But I needed to write you a letter, to save myself from me.

TRANSFORMATION

It started with a feeling deep down inside my heart.
Truth be told, it was a feeling I wanted to shake.
It was a feeling I couldn't quite place.
It was a feeling that made me feel sort of afraid.
It started with a feeling.

The feeling grew into an urge deep down inside my heart.
Truth be told, it was an urge I wanted to run from.
The urge was leading me in a direction I didn't want to go.
The urge led me into territory where I knew I wouldn't be
welcome
It grew into an urge.

The urge led to a yearning deep down inside my heart.
Truth be told, I was afraid of the things I was learning.
I was scared to tell people that I actually wanted to know.
I was afraid to follow a path that would force me to let go.
It grew into a yearning.

The yearning grew into desire deep down inside my heart.
Truth be told, I was starting to think a bit differently.
I was thinking that I was on to something sweet and
beautiful.
I was thinking that I was drawn to something good for me.
It grew into a desire.

The desire grew into belief deep down inside my heart.
Truth be told, my eyes were opened and my life began to change.
I walked a different walk and had an unashamed confession.
I talked a different talk and got a new and better direction.
And to think, it started with a feeling.

DEAR WORLD

Stay woke, Stay woke; open up your eyes,
The enemies are coming from every direction.
If the world is truth, then the truth is lies.

Hidden behind riches and glory as a prize,
they gives a façade of happiness and life perfection.
Stay woke, Stay woke; open up your eyes.

Falling through a dark hole they even hear your cries,
The world's ruler promises security and protection.
If the world is truth, then the truth is lies.

Shake it up, wake it up, see your life's demise.
Find the Truth and make the connection.
Stay woke, stay woke, open up your eyes.

See the light, feel the love, hear the wise.
Make a clear and appropriate inspection.
If the world is truth, then the truth is lies.

Don't let vanity and false sentiment be your demise.
Choose the clean, true, and right life selection.
Stay woke, stay woke open up your eyes.
If the world is truth, then the truth is lies.

QUESTIONS, COMMENTS, CONCERNS

To Whom It May Concern:

Excuse me, God? I need to talk to you. Are you there? Can
you hear my cries?
I know I'm new and you don't know me that well, but I
need to discuss my membership.
See, when the pastor was preaching that day, well… I guess
you know, you were there.
But he said I could lay my burdens on you and be freed
from the pain that I bear.
The deacons all stood there with open arms and they looked
like I could trust them.
So I walked up there, God. I had a feeling that I thought
came from you, so I walked up there.
But, um, I need to discuss my membership today. I know
I'm still within my 90 days.
I'm a little upset with the service I've been getting and
when I went to your people they told me that you were the
manager.

See, there's people in my life that have been sucking me
dry and I thought they would be gone when I became a
member. But they still here using me and taking me for
granted. They're still making me feel depressed and self-
conscious. They are still aggravating my anxiety and
abusing me. Where is the removal service that I thought
came with my membership?

Oh, and then there's the bills. The bills are still due, God. I
mean, ok, I knew the bills would still be due, but there's no

extra money coming through. I mean, I prayed for you to make a way just like they told me to, but I guess the way is blocked because all I see are words like "delinquent", "final notice", and "warning". This is a burden that I thought was eased with my membership.

And… I mean, I don't mean to be a complainer, I *do* appreciate the everlasting life thing. But I have these habits that you were supposed to break that remain unbroken. I tried to stop doing these things, but I can't seem to shake them. I thought you were going to help me out with that…

Oh and I definitely need you to make note of this. The whole reason I was drawn in was because of the love that everyone keeps talking about, but your existing members, Lord, I just can't figure out. I mean, they nice and all but some of them are rude. And some of them are demanding and some of them need.. well.. You. Don't get me wrong a lot of them are great, but they are quick to tell me what I should be doing, like I don't have enough on my plate. They keep telling me to come to this and that and want to talk to me about ministry, but I'm not laying my hands to do nothing until I get what I need for me!

God, with all due respect, I don't think I'm satisfied with the results I was promised. There's no joy or peace or patience or strength. I don't even think I've learned how to shout yet. Why aren't people admiring me for being this great person that chose the Lord? And where is this internal spirit that is supposed to guide me? I just don't think I got all of the parts of my package plan.

Sincerely Yours Through Christ.

● ●

To Whom It Should Concern:

Well, it's nice to finally hear from you my child, it has been
quite a while. I was hoping the next time we talked you'd
be coming with a smile. But I see you have some issues.
Yes, I could hear your crying quite well and I can tell
you're unhappy with the decision you think you've made.
Let me make it clear I know better than you do. I already
had an inkling that I'd soon be hearing from you. I knew
when you came down the aisle, you had a different point of
view, but I was hoping you'd be more open to what
blessings are in store for you.

I'm not sure what you're expecting nor of who's timetable
you think I'm on. But there's not trial period with this
membership, it's a lifetime commitment, or well, at least
that's what I ask. Yes, I am the manager and the
supervisor, and the owner, the creator, the conflict
resolution department, Human Resources (that's my
specialty), the CEO, CFO, COO, President, Founder… get
it? I'm sure I can help you with your complaints today.
Now, I hope you don't mind me calling them complaints,
but that's what they are. And truth is just my thing so sugar
coating won't be happening here.

Let's start with the people in your life. What exactly would
you like me to do? Should I come down and have a talk
with them on behalf of you? Would you like me to wipe
them out? Banish them to a far away land? What exactly do
you have planned? My child, your membership doesn't

27

come with a removal service that you thought it would, it comes with removal assistance, the service part is for you to do. You know who the people are who are bad for you, but it's been your choice to keep them around. So, its not for me to decide what you do down there on the ground. I showed you she was a snake and I showed you he was a liar. I even sent your friends and family to give you the truth you desire. But you are still dealing with these people. You are still in these social groups. Your membership gives you access to a whole new body of people who may give you a different experience.

I'm unsure why you have the inclination to believe your problems would just disappear, but I'll keep addressing your issues, since you seem to be unclear.

Your bills are your bills and how you pay them is up to you. I have some blessings lined up for you, but you are not yet ready to receive them. When your hands are closed to give, my child, then they're not open to receive and no matter how many opportunities I gave you, you kept them that way. Not only them, but your mouth hasn't witnessed your benefit of my goodness, your feet haven't carried anyone else's burdens, your lips haven't even offered up a sacrifice of praise, so your complaints are quite premature. Go to the job I blessed you with and pay your bills instead of... well, lets talk about those habits.

My child, again, it is not up to me to stop you from your negative habitual nature. That's the work you have to do. I am here to give you encouragement and strength, but you have to want it bad enough to do the work for you. But I'll let you in on a little secret since you think I've haven't been here. Remember when there was a mistake at the bank and it froze your accounts so you didn't have money for gas because you only had just enough to get to work? Yes, that kept you from driving to the habit you want me to instantly break for you and it caused you to momentarily forget about those urges. And then the next time you had them there was an emergency with your mom. Remember yelling at me about that? Well, she's fine now and your urge, that day, was gone. I know you refuse to see it, but your habits being around is not on me. I told you to lean this way, I want you to be free!

My people are rude and disrespectful, they're demanding and pushy? Hm. Seems you fit right in. The very things you say they are doing, are illustrated precisely in this complaint you've so eloquently written. There is a lot of love that I've seen you receive and much love is still to come. The goal for every member here is to reach the highest level of unconditional love possible. But have you shown them how to love? The unconditional love you are expecting to receive, are you giving? I'm not excusing rude behavior and not condoning disrespect, however you, as a member, have a duty to correct. Some are definitely legitimate and many are praying for help, but others are trying to help you with a truth that has a duty to offend.

My child, I love you and I always will. I am here for you and my spirit is inside you still. I'm pretty sure I know the problem and why you're feeling this way. You haven't read the manual you were given the on your first day. The manual is comprehensive, it tell you everything you need to know about your membership. In it you will find out where to receive your blessings along with what is expected of you. It will tell you exactly where to find love, joy, hope, and strength and how you can use it to equip you with everything you need to do for yourself. You can always refer to it when you have a question or get stuck, there is even an app for your convenience. It is very important you use your manual to guide your everyday life. It will teach you how to tap into the spirit that is inside of you and how to let it take control. Most importantly, listen very closely. It will teach you how to pray so next time you come, you'll come correct.

Sincerely Yours With Christ.

SHE WALKED AWAY

She never thought she could, so she didn't.
She never knew she had a voice, so she stayed silent.
She was never told her thoughts mattered, so she didn't give an opinion.
She never felt wanted, so she walked away.

Chains of "can't" left her feeling like a failure.
Chains of "silence" left her vulnerable to vultures.
Chains of "worthlessness" left her regarded as a doormat.
Chains of "loneliness" left her grasping for attention.

Then she found the book.
Then she found what she needed.
Then she ran to the cross.
Then she became free!

Paul told her that she can do all things through Christ.
And the song writer said she was fearfully and wonderfully made.
Matthew told her she was important, and that God will give her what she needs.
But it was Jesus that said, "Follow me", so she dropped her chains, and she walked His way.

PART TWO:

THE MIDDLE

SINNER SAVED BY GRACE

THE CALL

My husband called just to say hi.
To hear my voice, and at times to cry.
He called me to tell me about his successful day.
Or to tell me how things just weren't going his way.
My husband called and of course him I answered.

My mother called to check on me.
To tell me she's fine and hear the baby.
She called me to catch up on whatever she's missed.
To catch me up too and send us a kiss.
My mother called and of course her I answered.

My best friend called to tell me the news.
To tell me a joke, to sing me the blues.
She called me to chat, to dish, and to ponder.
To ask, and to think, and to laugh, and to wonder.
My best friend called and of course her I answered.

The bill collector called to set up a plan.
To yell at me about how poorly I've planned.
He called me to beg, to bargain, to force.
To talk to me til his voice became hoarse.
The bill collector called and of course I blocked the number.

The telemarketer called to sell me a phone.
Or a window, or a door, or a plant, or a drone.
They called me to convince me to give it a try.
They called me from Florida, Turkey, and Dubai.
The telemarketer called and of course I hung up.

God called me one day to show me the way.
To tell me to listen, to watch and to pray.
He called me to say what he had ready for me.
To tell me how to prepare for the journey.
He called me and I was afraid to answer.

God called me again to tell me I needed to surface.
To tell me it's time to live out my purpose.
He called me to do the work He has for me.
To tell them His truth, to help lead us free.
God called me and finally I've answered.
And we're *STILL* talking!

DEAR FLESH

Why do you betray me?
Why do you make me feel like a failure when life is at a high point?
Why do you make me doubt when I know God has it all figured out?
Why do you force me to think and say and do things that I will later regret?
Why do you betray me?

Every time I'm getting closer and closer to success, you begin to share your deepest and darkest disappointments in an effort to distract me and to create feelings of worthlessness.

Every time I get closer and closer to God you draw out these memories of when it was just me and you against everything.
You try to make me forget that it was God that got both of us to this point.
You try to make me forget that it was God that helped me to recognize you for who you are.

Every time I get closer and closer to good-for-me people you begin to lay brick to protect what? Who? You?!
You try to make me connect them with the others and you don't even give them a chance to show and prove.
Always sneaking behind every good thought with a "but" or an "if" or a "just in case" and your favorite the "don't put it past them".

You seem to be my worst enemy, but you're my best friend.
Only you understand the battles we fight, the danger we face, the responsibilities we assume.
Only you have been and will always truly be with me. So, why are you the one trying to hinder me?

I wrote you this letter to ask that we make a pact.
I never want to forget what we've been through, but I also don't want you bringing it back.

I'm done with the world.
I know ya'll are good friends, but I'm done with the world!
Stop trying to force us together.

I'm done with regret.
I know you still have some, but I'm done.
I'm moving forward to bigger and better and no matter what, my choices led me here so let's just let it go.

I'm done with revenge.
Look, I know they deserve it, but let's think about it...
what do WE deserve?
It's not up to us. I have to forgive, it's better for the both of us.

I'm done with addictions.
I know this one will be hard for you, but you should already know by now.

They won't be coming back.
I know it's been confusing because this isn't my first "I'm done"
But, you know it's been a while now, and there's no turning back.

Me, I love you.
I always have, but you have been a burden to me at points in our life.
This letter is to show you that we're in this together and I want to do this right.
I love you, Me.
I promise I do. And I'm sorry about those times when I didn't show it.
I'm sorry for the lies I told you.
I'm sorry for the choices that damaged us.
I'm sorry for trying to end you.

I've started a new beginning for us.
Where you have forgiven me and I have forgiven you.
I've started a new beginning for us.
And I need you to let me lead.
I need you to trust me to follow the right path.
I need you to welcome the spirit inside of us.
I've started a new beginning for us.
I've given God the reigns.

He demands confidence and boldness.
You have to get on board.
He demands righteousness and good judgement.
You have to get on board.

He demands truth and wisdom.
You have to get on board.
I love you, Me.
But I now have power over you, so you have to get on
board.

BUT GOD

Fear wanted me to cower into a ball of confusion, pain, and grief, and for a moment it succeeded.
Somehow the torment of fear felt comfortable and predictable.
But soon fear became anguish and anxiety. I cried late at night, early in the morning and in the height of noon.
My tears became a regular accompaniment to the constant thoughts of worst-case scenarios.

I became allergic to hope.

Hope was the mountaintop I'd proudly stood on until a strong wind came and knocked me back down to earth.
Hope was the well thought out plans for the future that were squashed with every new update.
Hope was the far away land that everyone else was privy to while I spent my days trying to figure out if it really existed.
Hope became a figment of the imagination, so my body rejected every notion of it and it left me cold and dehydrated.

Shivering and worn, I'd accepted my defeat.

Fear, Anxiety, and Hopelessness now my best friends, my true companions, my immediate resolve; led me to a dark maiden with open arms. Her name was Pity.
Pity reveled in being my rock bottom, but she was unaware of the power of God.
She sang the song over and over in my head of how the cards were stacked against me and how my family would

always see me as the secret mistake.
She danced to the beat of the constant drum of failure.

Boom. Relationships. Bada-Boom. Friendships. Boom-Bada-Boom. School. Boom-Boom. Christian.

She laughed at the thought of betrayal. Excited to bring it back to memory.
How he did and she did and that led me to there and now I'm here while they're there doing that for them and all the while I was everything to them and ended up with only heartbreak that led me to be, this.

But. God.

The introduction was familiar, but the voice was different, could it really be for me?

But. God.

The hope was apparent, but the goal seemed unreachable.

But. God.

The preparation was arduous but necessary. Could I complete this task?

But. God.

Hope is the mountaintop, I humbly stand on, recognizing that only God can keep me rooted.
Strong winds can't knock me off, but sometimes I meet God in the valley for character building exercises.

Hope is the blessed assurance that God is in control.
No matter what comes my way, plans established by God
can never be crushed.

Hope is where I dwell and where my faith is realized.
Hope is the reality of victory in Christ.
Hope is the inspiration of purpose.
Hope is the warmth of love wrapped in mercy and sealed
with grace.

Because. God.

OVERCOMER

Who said I wouldn't make it?

The words were loud and clear printed on her shirt in glittery letters.

Wouldn't make it past what I wondered?

What have you gone through where people doubted your survival or held secret hopes of your failure?

Who dared to believe they were privy to your destination when they couldn't even understand that you are not even under your own direction?

Who said I wouldn't make it?

The words were loud and clear coming from her lips.

Wouldn't make it where I wondered.

What obstacles were placed in your path to disrupt your goals and hopes for the future?

Who dared to believe that they could put out your fire when the fire you possess is not even your own?

Who said you wouldn't make it?

Who said I wouldn't make it?

Who said we wouldn't make it?

They all did.

They whispered it in your ear every time the test results told you this torture wasn't over.

They threw it in your face every time you thought you could walk away.

They shouted it behind your back as soon as they hung up the phone from telling you it would all work out.

They screamed it out loud whenever their prayers for you turned into hopeless pleading for what they think is peace.

Even you did.

When your fear arose and your courage failed. You said you wouldn't make it.

When my hope dissipated and my power depleted. I said I wouldn't make it.

When we allowed those words to play on repeat. When we ate them for every meal. We said we wouldn't make it.

But, who said God wouldn't do it?

No one could and no one will because he always does.

He did it and we made it.

He's doing it and we're making it.

When fear rises, courage rises higher because the Lord is our light and our salvation; whom shall we fear?

When misplaced hope begins to fail, we are reminded to place it in the Lord, for then will our strength be renewed and we remember the power that we possess.

Who said you wouldn't make it? You are an overcomer.

Who said I wouldn't make it? I am an overcomer.

Who said we wouldn't make it? With God, we all are overcomers!

I DON'T KNOW HOW TO PRAISE YOU

I don't know how to praise you.
I can give you shouts of Glory! Hallelujah! Praise your
Name!
But my shouting doesn't feel good enough when I think
of from whence my help came.

I don't know how to praise you.
I can sing from my soul in pure delight, just how
wonderful you are.
But even if the angels were impressed, my melodies
would still be sub-par

I don't know how to praise you.
I can dance a holy dance of praise to express my
gratitude.
But my strongest expression, nor smoothest flow could
match the praise you're due.

I don't know how to praise you.
I can walk a life worth mentioning when we speak of
following your lead.
But I can't be good enough to bring you the glory you
deserve through act or deed.

I don't know how to praise you.
Sometimes I feel ashamed because you deserve more
praise than I know how to give.
But I praise the best I can because you're the only
reason why I live.

I don't know how to praise you.
Your love is so deep and so true and I'm just a wretch
trying to give you what's due.
But the most amazing thing about your love is you still
accept my praise even though,

I don't know how to praise you.

PART THREE:

THE PURPOSE

THE GREAT COMMISSION

DEAR YOU

Hey you! Yeah, you! This letter is for you!
Not the you I can see, but for the you that is true.

For the you that feels ashamed, with a heart full of
regretful grief,
This letter is to tell you; God's forgiveness is your
relief.

For the you that feels hurt, your mind and soul
riddled with pain,
This letter is for you, a little sunshine to break up
your rain.

For the you that has no hope, who has lost all desire
and faith,
This letter is for you, to lead you back to an
encouraging place.

For the you that can't find help, and you don't know
where to turn,
This letter is especially for you, an answer to your
concern.

Hey you!

You are important! Let's start with that basic fact.
Your life is valuable, your company desired, so that
doubt you can subtract.

You are worth love and affection. You are worthy to be treated well.
You do not have to settle for damages to your mental and physical health.

You are forgiven. Even if you've never even apologized.
In the love of Christ, you are forgiven. Don't believe the devil's lies.

You are truly forgiven. Let's back it up. Let me reiterate the notion.
God's grace and mercy releases you from the guilty mind's commotion.

You'll always deserve better, until the best is what you get.
So keep striving to reach higher, because you haven't reached the top yet.

You are in control of your destiny. Your future is in your command.
The best choice you'll ever make is to rest it all in God's hands.

You are smarter than you know. And your thinking is quick and deep.
But in order to tap into wisdom, you must wake out of your sleep.

Your potential has no end. Your power has no ceiling to reach.
Don't limit your life's possibilities to the world's restraining speech.

This letter is for you. Yeah you! The one whose faith has waned.
Christ is calling, He's waiting, He's standing there. With the blood that will keep you sustained.

DON'T FORGET ABOUT GOD

The days are filled with pain and nightfall only
intensifies the grief.
The only hope left is reserved for slumber that will
bring some temporary relief.

The mind is clouded with what ifs and thoughts of
what to do.
And with the strength that seems to be left, the only
resolve is to just push through.

But soon the cloudy days give way and the light of
better times arrive.
Circumstances improve, solution come into view,
and the world never felt more alive.

The people are relieved and with happiness, they
shout and cheer and applaud.
But, the victory is not sustained in their hearts
because they forgot all about God.

Where was the faith when the trouble was deep, and
the darkness shielded the escape?
Where was hope placed when fear had to be faced
and the worry kept them awake?

The security that comes with true joy was bogged
down with the distress if uncertainty.
The weakness of self-reliance only left you with a
façade of successful normalcy.

When the period of trials passed and the tears were
wiped away, where were your shouts of praise?
Where was your testimony shared? Where was your
witness revealed? Why was thanksgiving delayed?

Mountain highs and valley lows all have a journey
in between.
And the way you bear the journey forth is knowing
on whom to lean.

Not matter where you are in life, know your victory
and joy can go with you wherever you trod.
But only as long as you know where your help
come from and you don't forget about God.

CHANGE YOUR MIND

Jesus is the way and truth and the light.
If you think otherwise, you don't have it right.
No time for games, to be nice and polite,
In the middle of a war you need to fight

Don't get me wrong, Jesus doesn't need you to win.
The point here is for you to be freed from your sin.
Then you can see the battle you probably didn't
know you were in.
And your defense can be stronger because your
victory lies within.

You don't know when your last breath's in line.
The offer is salvation, please don't decline.
Jesus is the only way to stop being blind.
Give Him your heart and He'll Change Your Mind!

LET ME LEAD YOU

Let me lead you to the altar where Christ led me.
To the power of the Lord to set my soul free.
Where a new life awaits for you to receive,
Where you lay your burdens down and come up
able to breathe.

Let me lead you to the river where Christ led me.
To the wide-open waters where He made me clean.
Where the water takes your sin and washes it away,
Where a fresh and renewed spirit leads you to a
brighter day.

Let me lead you to the church where Christ led me.
To the place of strength and knowledge where He
nourishes me.
Where praises go up in unison and blessings never
subside.
Where your thirst and hunger for knowledge is
always satisfied.

Let me lead to you the savior like it was done for
me.
To the one who gave me joy, love, hope, and peace.
Where you walk a new walk of righteousness and a
grace and mercy abounds.
Let me lead you to the savior where true life is
found.

THE LAYOVER

Praise the Lord! And thank you for traveling with me! You haven't reached the end, just a layover because, well, the journey isn't over is it? I mean, think about it… reading this book was a part of your journey. Now, this part of your journey is over and it's time to get off this ride and hop on to the next one.

I really hope that, like the journey of life, this book made you think, enlightened your spirit, upset you at times, gave you joy, and broadened your thinking. At the very least, I hope you enjoyed something you read. My deepest prayer is that your life was somehow impacted by the words and the spirit behind the words.

I will keep you all in my prayers and I hope you continue to pray for me too. I'll leave you with one last bonus poem. A worship poem to our God.

I love you! God loves you more! So, love him back! Peace.

HALLELUJAH, LORD

Hallelujah, Lord.
All glory and honor belong to you.
For, from nothing you created it all.
So, all praise and worship is due.

Hallelujah, Lord.
Your magnificence knows no bounds
We lift up hands of praise
In your presence we bow down

Hallelujah Lord.
We bless your name on high
We thank you for being you
Of your goodness, we testify.

Hallelujah Lord.
We will praise you 'til our last breath
Then we will look forward to shouting Hallelujah
In the eternity after death.

Made in the USA
Monee, IL
21 March 2021

62494260R00035